This Notebook Belongs to :

D1571495

_____

INFORMATION:

Name: _____

DOB: _____ Gender: _____

Breed:	Vet Clinic:
Color:	Insurance#:
Microchip #:	Doctor:
Allergies:	Clinic Phone:

Date:	Age:	Vaccine:	Note:

FEEDING LOG:

Date:	Time:	Food:	Amount (%):

Notes:

FEEDING LOG:

Date:	Time:	Food:	Amount (%):

Notes:

FEEDING LOG:

Date:	Time:	Food:	Amount (%):

Notes:

FEEDING LOG:

Date:	Time:	Food:	Amount (%):

Notes:

FEEDING LOG:

Date:	Time:	Food:	Amount (%):

Notes:

FEEDING LOG:

Date:	Time:	Food:	Amount (%):

Notes:

FEEDING LOG:

Date:	Time:	Food:	Amount (%):

Notes:

FEEDING LOG:

Date:	Time:	Food:	Amount (%):

Notes:

FEEDING LOG:

Date:	Time:	Food:	Amount (%):

Notes:

WALKING LOG:

Date:	Time:	Walker:	Notes:
	AM/PM		
	AM/PM		
	AM/PM		
	AM/PM		
	AM/PM		
	AM/PM		
	AM/PM		
	AM/PM		
	AM/PM		
	AM/PM		
	AM/PM		
	AM/PM		

Notes:

WALKING LOG:

Date:	Time:	Walker:	Notes:
	AM/PM		
	AM/PM		
	AM/PM		
	AM/PM		
	AM/PM		
	AM/PM		
	AM/PM		
	AM/PM		
	AM/PM		
	AM/PM		
	AM/PM		
	AM/PM		

Notes:

WALKING LOG:

Date:	Time:	Walker:	Notes:
	AM/PM		
	AM/PM		
	AM/PM		
	AM/PM		
	AM/PM		
	AM/PM		
	AM/PM		
	AM/PM		
	AM/PM		
	AM/PM		
	AM/PM		
	AM/PM		

Notes:

WALKING LOG:

Date:	Time:	Walker:	Notes:
	AM/PM		
	AM/PM		
	AM/PM		
	AM/PM		
	AM/PM		
	AM/PM		
	AM/PM		
	AM/PM		
	AM/PM		
	AM/PM		
	AM/PM		
	AM/PM		

Notes:

WALKING LOG:

Date:	Time:	Walker:	Notes:
	AM/PM		
	AM/PM		
	AM/PM		
	AM/PM		
	AM/PM		
	AM/PM		
	AM/PM		
	AM/PM		
	AM/PM		
	AM/PM		
	AM/PM		
	AM/PM		

Notes:

WALKING LOG:

Date:	Time:	Walker:	Notes:
	AM/PM		
	AM/PM		
	AM/PM		
	AM/PM		
	AM/PM		
	AM/PM		
	AM/PM		
	AM/PM		
	AM/PM		
	AM/PM		
	AM/PM		
	AM/PM		

Notes:

WALKING LOG:

Date:	Time:	Walker:	Notes:
	AM/PM		
	AM/PM		
	AM/PM		
	AM/PM		
	AM/PM		
	AM/PM		
	AM/PM		
	AM/PM		
	AM/PM		
	AM/PM		
	AM/PM		
	AM/PM		

Notes:

WALKING LOG:

Date:	Time:	Walker:	Notes:
	AM/PM		
	AM/PM		
	AM/PM		
	AM/PM		
	AM/PM		
	AM/PM		
	AM/PM		
	AM/PM		
	AM/PM		
	AM/PM		
	AM/PM		
	AM/PM		

Notes:

WALKING LOG:

Date:	Time:	Walker:	Notes:
	AM/PM		
	AM/PM		
	AM/PM		
	AM/PM		
	AM/PM		
	AM/PM		
	AM/PM		
	AM/PM		
	AM/PM		
	AM/PM		
	AM/PM		
	AM/PM		

Notes:

WALKING LOG:

Date:	Time:	Walker:	Notes:
	AM/PM		
	AM/PM		
	AM/PM		
	AM/PM		
	AM/PM		
	AM/PM		
	AM/PM		
	AM/PM		
	AM/PM		
	AM/PM		
	AM/PM		
	AM/PM		

Notes:

WALKING LOG:

Date:	Time:	Walker:	Notes:
	AM/PM		
	AM/PM		
	AM/PM		
	AM/PM		
	AM/PM		
	AM/PM		
	AM/PM		
	AM/PM		
	AM/PM		
	AM/PM		
	AM/PM		
	AM/PM		

Notes:

WALKING LOG:

Date:	Time:	Walker:	Notes:
	AM/PM		
	AM/PM		
	AM/PM		
	AM/PM		
	AM/PM		
	AM/PM		
	AM/PM		
	AM/PM		
	AM/PM		
	AM/PM		
	AM/PM		
	AM/PM		

Notes:

WALKING LOG:

Date:	Time:	Walker:	Notes:
	AM/PM		
	AM/PM		
	AM/PM		
	AM/PM		
	AM/PM		
	AM/PM		
	AM/PM		
	AM/PM		
	AM/PM		
	AM/PM		
	AM/PM		
	AM/PM		

Notes:

WALKING LOG:

Date:	Time:	Walker:	Notes:
	AM/PM		
	AM/PM		
	AM/PM		
	AM/PM		
	AM/PM		
	AM/PM		
	AM/PM		
	AM/PM		
	AM/PM		
	AM/PM		
	AM/PM		
	AM/PM		

Notes:

GROWTH TRACKER:

Date:	Age:	Weight:	Height:

Notes:

GROWTH TRACKER:

Date:	Age:	Weight:	Height:

Notes:

GROWTH TRACKER:

Date:	Age:	Weight:	Height:

Notes:

GROWTH TRACKER:

Date:	Age:	Weight:	Height:

Notes:

GROWTH TRACKER:

Date:	Age:	Weight:	Height:

Notes:

GROOMING LOG:

Date:	Groomer:	Treatment:	Cost:

Notes:

GROOMING LOG:

Date:	Groomer:	Treatment:	Cost:

Notes:

GROOMING LOG:

Date:	Groomer:	Treatment:	Cost:

Notes:

GROOMING LOG:

Date:	Groomer:	Treatment:	Cost:

Notes:

GROOMING LOG:

Date:	Groomer:	Treatment:	Cost:

Notes:

GROOMING LOG:

Date:	Groomer:	Treatment:	Cost:

Notes:

GROOMING LOG:

Date:	Groomer:	Treatment:	Cost:

Notes:

GROOMING LOG:

Date:	Groomer:	Treatment:	Cost:

Notes:

GROOMING LOG:

Date:	Groomer:	Treatment:	Cost:

Notes:

GROOMING LOG:

Date:	Groomer:	Treatment:	Cost:

Notes:

TRAINING LOG:

DATE: _____

LESSON: _____

TRAINER: _____

Material Used:

Lesson Points:

Lesson Notes:

TRAINING LOG:

DATE: _____

LESSON: _____

TRAINER: _____

Material Used:

Lesson Points:

Lesson Notes:

TRAINING LOG:

DATE: _____

LESSON: _____

TRAINER: _____

Material Used:

Lesson Points:

Lesson Notes:

TRAINING LOG:

DATE: _____

LESSON: _____

TRAINER: _____

Material Used:

Lesson Points:

Lesson Notes:

TRAINING LOG:

DATE: _____

LESSON: _____

TRAINER: _____

Material Used:

Lesson Points:

Lesson Notes:

TRAINING LOG:

DATE: _____

LESSON: _____

TRAINER: _____

Material Used:

Lesson Points:

Lesson Notes:

TRAINING LOG:

DATE: _____

LESSON: _____

TRAINER: _____

Material Used:

Lesson Points:

Lesson Notes:

TRAINING LOG:

DATE: _____

LESSON: _____

TRAINER: _____

Material Used:

Lesson Points:

Lesson Notes:

TRAINING LOG:

DATE: _____

LESSON: _____

TRAINER: _____

Material Used:

Lesson Points:

Lesson Notes:

TRAINING LOG:

DATE: _____

LESSON: _____

TRAINER: _____

Material Used:

Lesson Points:

Lesson Notes:

APPOINTMENTS:

Date:	Age:	Appointment:	Reason:

Notes:

APPOINTMENTS:

Date:	Age:	Appointment:	Reason:

Notes:

APPOINTMENTS:

Date:	Age:	Appointment:	Reason:

Notes:

APPOINTMENTS:

Date:	Age:	Appointment:	Reason:

Notes:

APPOINTMENTS:

Date:	Age:	Appointment:	Reason:

Notes:

MEDICATIONS:

Date:	Medication:	Dose:	Time:

Notes:

MEDICATIONS:

Date:	Medication:	Dose:	Time:

Notes:

MEDICATIONS:

Date:	Medication:	Dose:	Time:

Notes:

MEDICATIONS:

Date:	Medication:	Dose:	Time:

Notes:

MEDICATIONS:

Date:	Medication:	Dose:	Time:

Notes:

MEDICATIONS:

Date:	Medication:	Dose:	Time:

Notes:

MEDICATIONS:

Date:	Medication:	Dose:	Time:

Notes:

MEDICATIONS:

Date:	Medication:	Dose:	Time:

Notes:

MEMORIES:

Date:
Description:

MEMORIES:

Date:
Description:

MEMORIES:

Date:
Description:

MEMORIES:

Date:
Description:

MEMORIES:

Date:
Description:

MEMORIES:

Date:
Description:

MEMORIES:

Date:
Description:

MEMORIES:

Date:
Description:

MEMORIES:

Date:
Description:

MEMORIES:

Date:
Description:

MEMORIES:

Date:
Description:

MEMORIES:

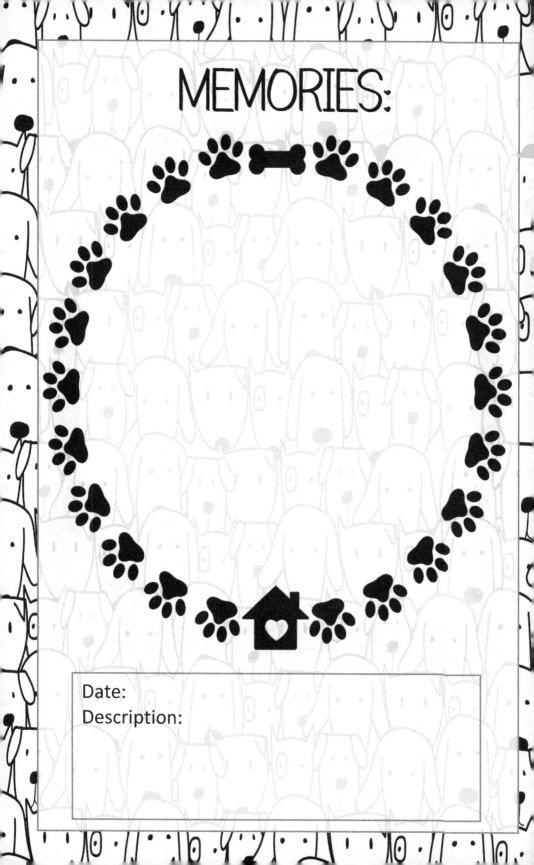

Date:
Description:

MEMORIES:

Date:
Description:

MEMORIES:

Date:
Description:

MEMORIES:

Date:
Description:

MEMORIES:

Date:
Description:

MEMORIES:

Date:
Description:

MEMORIES:

Date:
Description:

MEMORIES:

Date:
Description:

MEMORIES:

Date:
Description:

MEMORIES:

Date:
Description:

MEMORIES:

Date:
Description:

MEMORIES:

Date:
Description:

MEMORIES:

Date:
Description:

PURCHASE LOG:

DATE	STORE	ITEM	COST	LIKE/DISLIKE

Notes:

PURCHASE LOG:

DATE	STORE	ITEM	COST	LIKE/DISLIKE

Notes:

PURCHASE LOG:

DATE	STORE	ITEM	COST	LIKE/DISLIKE

Notes:

PURCHASE LOG:

DATE	STORE	ITEM	COST	LIKE/DISLIKE

Notes:

PURCHASE LOG:

DATE	STORE	ITEM	COST	LIKE/DISLIKE

Notes:

PURCHASE LOG:

DATE	STORE	ITEM	COST	LIKE/DISLIKE

Notes:

HOTEL/BOARDING:

PLACE:	DATE IN:	DATE OUT:	COST:

HOTEL/BOARDING:

PLACE:	DATE IN:	DATE OUT:	COST:

HOTEL/BOARDING:

PLACE:	DATE IN:	DATE OUT:	COST:

HOTEL/BOARDING:

PLACE:	DATE IN:	DATE OUT:	COST:

CONTACTS:

NAME:	COMPANY:	NUMBER:	NOTE:

CONTACTS:

NAME:	COMPANY:	NUMBER:	NOTE:

Made in the USA
Monee, IL
17 June 2022

98173703R00057